Nicola Ama

NRDBMS
(Non-Relational Database Management System)

Technologies

What they are and how they bring strategic advantages
exploiting corporate digital assets.

The case studies of three famous databases used by
Amazon, Google and Facebook.

———————————————

Research project based on a proposal submitted to
University of Derby (UK) in 2012

———————————————

Table of contents

Abstract

The intention of this research project is to investigate an innovative topic concerning a new system, which is implemented to manage databases based on a non-relational model.

This work has been structured in a way that any reader can smoothly be introduced to the non-relational databases problematic.

Firstly, there is an overview of NRDBMSs and their implementation methods (columnfamily, document store, graph, key/value, etc.). Then, a picture of advantages and disadvantages of non-relational databases is drawn.

Furthermore, there is the description of some of the most NRDBMS technologies used by big companies and an explanation of their features (cloud technology, horizontal scaling, etc.) and eventually it is analysed how this technology could bring general advantages to business.

After having discussed this topic in general terms, there is the analysis of three particular case studies. The first two cases (Amazon and Google) are based on DB applications implemented on purpose by software houses, upon Amazon and Google requests (proprietary software). The third one (Facebook) is a commercial public domain software also used by Digg, Twitter, Rackspace.

Particularly, Amazon case study deals with the implementation of SimpleDB, a distributed database, its cloud technology, its key/value approach for storing data, benefit of eventual consistency use. Google case study regards the simplified interface of APP Engine Data Store that works on Blg Tables, the solidity of its database, its difference with Amazon SimpleDB. Finally, Facebook case study talks about Cassandra, the most famous NRDBMS used to manage huge and complex amount of data, its main characteristics such as horizontal scaling, independence of network nodes, redundancy

Last consideration to be taken is that for every single case there is first a general overview of NRDBMS technology used, and then most of the time is dedicated to talk about strategic advantages brought to exploit corporate digital assets.

Introduction

Lately, non-relational databases (NRDMS) have exponentially increased their popularity thanks mostly to the ever-increasing need to scale horizontally, a feature that the classic RDBMS has showed so far to have several limitations. Also because, managing an environment with RDBMS, where for instance cloud systems start to have a remarkable growth, it gets very complicated and the computational power is not optimally exploited. This is the main reason why big companies that usually manage databases with impressive amount of data decided to contribute to the development and implementation of Non-relational database management systems, grouped under the movement NoSQL (Not Only SQL).

1
Problem Formulation

1.1 Background

Relational database management systems have been so far the predominant technology for storing structured data. However, as it has been noticed that corporate data are growing very fast and on a daily base, and in some cases the relational model has showed some limitations, a more complex database management is felt as an urgent matter. Here is the idea to implement something different from SQL, more flexible and not strictly related to rigid relations. Thus, the concept of non-relational databases grew more and more since 1998, when Carlo Strozzi firstly used the term "NoSQL" to name his lightweight, open-source relational database not associated to any SQL interface.

But what actually are NRDBMS and what are the different key elements compared to the traditional way to manage databases?

NRDBMSs adopt a different concept about database management, more flexible and more capable to manage huge amount of data easily and faster. Its data stores, for instance, do not require fixed table schemas and usually avoid JOIN operations. Furthermore, in contrast to relational database management systems, most NoSQL databases are designed to scale well in the horizontal direction and not rely on highly available hardware. The most important is that non-relational databases provide a significant higher data throughput than traditional relational databases.

The main NRDBMS methods of implementation are the followings:

Coloumnfamily: data are organized into rows and columns, but rows can have as many columns is needed without any limit and is also no necessary to define columns firstly.

Document store: it can be considered the evolution of key/value method that, compared to the standard relational databases, instead of storing data into tables with fixed fields, these are put into a document that can contain unlimited fields of unlimited length. A clear explanatory case could be if, for instance, we only know the first and last name of a person, but we know more data about another different person, such as address, date of birth and Social Security number. With this method we can avoid that for the first person there are unused fields that take up unnecessary space.

Graph: data are stored as a graph structure; this way access to object-oriented applications is more powerful with higher performances.

Key/Value: in this case data are stored into an element that contains also a key along with current data.

What are pros and cons of non-relational databases?

Advantages.

As every single element contains all necessary information, there is no need to use the JOIN command, usually very wasteful in terms of performance, as it happens with relational databases.

Simplicity is the key element of these databases, as horizontal scaling is very efficient and allows adding nodes in an imperceptible way to the final user.

Choosing a database suitable for mapping directly applications object classes, can greatly reduce the time dedicated to the development of the method of exchanging data between the database and the application itself (the so-called object-relational mapping that is necessary in the presence of relational databases).

Disadvantages.

The fact that NRDBMSs are so simple to use and manage, however, can also lead to a lack of data integrity basic checks. Therefore, this task has to be performed by the application that in this case communicates with the database, which would obviously be very thoroughly tested before being put into production. For example, if we have a database of customers with their orders stored in different elements, even if it is possible to define a relationship through the keys, if we delete a customer from NRDBMS it happens that all his related orders would remain in the database; thus, is the application itself that has to delete both customer and related data, something that in a relational database is managed directly by the database itself.

The lack of a universal standard, like SQL, is another pitfall of these non-relational databases. In fact, every database has its own API and its method of storing and accessing data. Having said that, it comes natural to understand that if the development of the database on which we based our application is stopped for any reason, a switch to another database would certainly not be an immediate thing, but some radical changes would be necessary to be made to the application. Therefore, it would be worthwhile considering the matter at the initial brainstorming and, anyhow, before starting the implementation.

1.2 Literature Review

Notwithstanding database gurus commenced to talk about non-relational databases very long time ago, only nowadays, also due to the fact technology runs faster, there is an urgent need to go beyond RDBMS capabilities. High performances have been given by NoSQL databases, because they showed to be capable, unlike relational databases, to handle unstructured data such as word-processing files, e-mail, multimedia, and social media efficiently (Levitt, 2010).

Most of database researchers agree to the fact that the primary advantage of non-relational databases is their efficiency storing and manipulating huge quantities of data, demonstrating a good flexibility to data structure, as they scale well as data grows. Furthermore, it seems they are flexible enough to deal with semi-structured and sparse data sets (Tiwari, 2011).

Thus, NRDBMS technologies seem now are throwing down the gauntlet to the traditional database management based on JOIN relations. But Levitt (2010) asks what about non-relational databases limitations, margin of improvements, concerns, doubts? Many are the questions around this issue, as well as diversity of views is widespread. There is then a kind of euphoria from the most enthusiastic fans of NoSQL databases, but in the mean time we notice the presence of followers of a school of thought oriented toward scepticism about this new technology. Literature about this topic, therefore, is really crowded enough. There are papers concerning purely technical differences between SQL and NoSQL, such as the excellent work of Stonebraker (2010), but also books wider explanatory, like the one written by Reese (2009) where he tries to clarify the situation explaining brilliantly the differences between traditional deployment and cloud computing, stressing the fact that non-relational database application architectures have proved to be more efficient, even if not without some limitation, especially for what concern data consistency in particular cases.

Finally, from the problem formulation perspective, Roebuck (2011) fully agrees on Reese (2009) points of view, highlighting also the rise of NoSQL stores and their use to serve up data to online users and the effective possibility to allow access to files from multiple hosts sharing via a computer network.

1.3 Exploratory research

As mentioned in the previous paragraph, specific literature concerning non-relational databases theme is pretty large, and usually when a topic is so widely documented, basically it means there is a general interest around it. But there is also an elevated risk factor when many people have something to say around a subject: to meet several fake pieces of information, incorrect and imprecise. That's why I privileged in my research mainly only documents coming from referenced sources, such as official database libraries and papers and books approved by academic institutions, and for obvious reasons I avoided to reference my work with uncertain Web sites and dubious sources of information.

1.4 Aims and Objectives

Current research is aimed to focus on acquiring as much as possible information about non-relational databases, state of the art of NRDBMS, how far its technology went. Furthermore, another important aim of my work is to understand how non-relational databases differ from the traditional relational management and realize how much they are more efficient than them in terms of pure and complete database management and in which case they are not.

Once achieved this, my objectives are oriented towards the demonstration of how non-relational databases management system brings strategic advantages exploiting corporate digital assets.

For a better achievement of my goals I will take the opportunity also to add to my reading and studying an excellent technical paper written by Rasmus (2008), Director of Business Insights of Microsoft Corporation, where he describes IT as a strategic asset when implemented and used appropriately. Very meaningful is his assertion: *"Information technology becomes a strategic asset when it makes the entire business adaptive and ready for change"* (Rasmus, 2008).

Another interesting job that I will deeply examine is the book of Taniar (2009), in which he discusses developments in data mining and warehousing as well as techniques for successful implementation. Also because, already at the first sight this book shows how useful foundation it can be for academicians and practitioners to research new techniques and methodologies.

In conclusion, since my research is not intended to be merely a theoretical paper, a considerable part of my job will be dedicated to analyse the strategic improvements assets of several cases of companies that actually switched to NRDBMS. In this context, three case studies will be analysed with particular meticulousness.

2
Research Methods Review

A vast majority of the information gathered for this proposed study will consist principally of books and papers coming from referenced and official sources, evaluated also by experts as trustable and reliable sources of quality information. As secondary means of information, journals, internet, and newspaper articles will be choose to integrate my research, whether of course they will be considered to be consistent.

The same ideological approach has been utilised to methodology I adopted.

In particular, analysing the majority of methods used by different researchers of NRDBMS topic, it appears that the most used method is the empirical research that tests the achievability of a solution based on empirical evidences, and obviously founded exclusively on quantitative methodology for the investigation system perspective. Nevertheless, my intention will be firstly the adoption of a mixed investigation system which includes also a qualitative research in order to understand also human behaviours towards strategic benefits of non-relational database systems (Creswell, 2002). I will also dedicate some time to develop some exploratory research in order to identify new problems related to the use of non-relational databases and, whether possible, I will implement also a constructive research for developing and suggesting solutions to problems I identified with the exploratory method. For this last task, and for the whole research project setting, I will get technical support from an outstanding book written by Oates (2006).

3
Research Design

For what concern my research design, after having covered all problem formulation topic, where general background of what non-relational databases are and their related implementation methods, other than the coverage of advantages and disadvantages, there will be a description of some of the most NRDBMS technologies used by big companies and what are their features (cloud technology, horizontal scaling, etc.) and how this technology could bring general advantages to business. However, this work would be considered pretty generalist if particular cases were not tackled. Therefore, going deeper into the problematic, I noticed that there were many options to be chosen among all corporations involved in NRDBMS. After a close evaluation my decision dropped on three cases, both due to the fact they brilliantly cover the two main kinds of application database implementations, the proprietary software and the public domain one, and also because the three major world companies on Internet are involved. And if companies like Google, Facebook and Amazon decide to switch to a non-relational database, there must be valuable reasons for this.

Obviously, the three cases I would like to discuss are the followings:

- Amazon case study: the implementation of SimpleDB, a distributed database, its cloud technology, its key/value approach for storing data and benefit of eventual consistency use (Habeeb, 2010);

- Google case study: the simplified interface of APP Engine Data Store that works on Blg Tables, the solidity of its database, its difference with Amazon SimpleDB (Sanderson, 2009);

- Facebook case study: Cassandra, the most famous NRDBMS used to manage huge and complex amount of data, its main characteristics such as horizontal scaling, independence of network nodes, redundancy (Hevitt, 2010).

For every single case there will be first a general overview explanation of the NRDBMS technology used. However, most of the time will be spent to talk about strategic advantages brought to exploit corporate digital assets. The first 2 cases (Amazon and Google) are based on DB applications implemented on purpose by software houses upon Amazon and Google requests (proprietary software). The third one (Facebook) is a commercial public domain software also used by Digg, Twitter, Rackspace.

4
Research Limitations

At a first sight and general evaluation, I do not see any major problem concerning limitations can arise whilst on implementation of my research project. However, I am strongly under the impression that exploratory and constructive methods, which I declared to adopt as well, might need a closer supervision by my side. In fact, I am convinced that, whatever is the field in subject, identifying new problems and developing and suggesting solutions never is easy, and can always give hard time to find out the key of the problem.

In order to mitigate that risk, my approach to every single topic related to NRDBMS, even to very small ones, will be with the awareness that, among all aspects to analyse there will be also space and time to dedicate to discover new probable problems and find related possible solutions. For what concerns existing problems, my intention is to focus on the most evident and declared issues and to test by myself, in a different system environment than the previous used ones, in order to analyse and revise their behaviours.

5
Amazon case study: the implementation of SimpleDB

What Amazon SimpleDB is?

It is a distributed database written in Erlang, a general-purpose programming language and runtime system designed by Ericsson, implemented by Amazon.com. It is used as a web service in concert with Amazon Elastic Compute Cloud EC2, that allows users to rent virtual computers on which to run their own computer applications, and the online storage web service Amazon S3 as a part of Amazon Web Services.

Basically, SimpleDB is a hosted cloud-based web service which comes up with a challenging alternative to the conventional relational databases that we normally use. It follows a streamlined approach by providing only the core functionality for storing and querying data for all complex and ambiguous operations frequently found in a traditional database system. And as it's based on XML, it gives the possibility to store data quickly and retrieve or edit them through a simple set of web service API through any programming language and platform.

Actually, SimpleDB is considered to be the most valuable data storage solution for building new web applications. This because it routinely carries out many day to day jobs associated with management and scalability of database.

What are its advantages?

Firstly I would mention the possibility of having really large data sets and it's really fast and highly available. Other positive points are the fact it's on demand scaling, like S3, EC2, with a sensible data metering pricing model; it's also schema-less, very important factor, where items are little hash tables containing sets of key, value pairs. In few words, it means that SimpleDB differently from any relational database where the priority is the definition of a schema for each database table before using it and where it's necessary to clearly change that schema before storing data differently. In SimpleDB, there is not at all any schema requirement. Even though data format are to be taken in consideration, this approach has the benefit of freeing you from the time it takes to manage schema modifications.

However, there are some considerations to be made about some disadvantages: eventual consistency for instance. In practical terms it means data is not immediately propagated across all nodes; the latency is usually around a second, but for high data sets or loads you may experience more latency. On the plus side, your data isn't lost!

Another issue may be represented by queries as they are lexis-graphical. Thus, you'll need to store data in lexicographical ordered form (zero-pad your integers, add positive offsets to negative integer sets, and convert dates into something like ISO 8601)

Moreover, also search indexes may be a problem. This means you will need to construct your own indexes for text search. The SimpleDB query expressions don't support text search, so you'll have to construct inverted indexes to properly do "text search". This is actually a really great lightweight way to do this and I'm sure many interesting indexing schemes will be possible.

However, considering that data model is simply a large collections of items organized into domains, and also that items are little hash tables containing attributes of key, value pairs, and finally that attributes can be searched with various lexicographical queries, now we can easily build search indexes, log databases / analysis tools, data mining stores, tools for World Domination.

Definitely, SimpleDB is a great innovation in the world of database concept and a very useful tool.

6
Google case study: the simplified interface of APP Engine Data Store

App Engine is a service offered by Google written in Java or Python used for developing and hosting web applications in Google-managed data centers. As an application-hosting platform, App Engine includes many non-database functions, but the App Engine data store has similarities to SimpleDB. The non-database functions include a number of different services, all of which are available via API calls. The APIs include service calls to Memcached, email, XMPP, and URL fetching.

App Engine includes an API for data storage based on Google Big Table and in some ways is comparable to SimpleDB. Although Big Table is not directly accessible to App Engine applications, there is support in the data store API for a number of features not available in

SimpleDB. These features include data relations, object mapping, transactions, and a user-defined index for each query.

App Engine also has a number of restrictions, some of which are similar to SimpleDB restrictions, like query run time. By default, the App Engine data store is strongly consistent. Once a transaction commits, all subsequent reads will reflect the changes in that transaction. It also means that if the primary storage node you are using goes down, App Engine will fail any update attempts you make until a suitable replacement takes over. To alleviate this issue, App Engine has recently added support for the same type of eventual consistency that SimpleDB has had all along. This move in the direction of SimpleDB gives App Engine apps the same ability as SimpleDB apps to run with strong consistency with option to fall back on eventual consistency to continue with a degraded level of service.

7
Facebook case study: Cassandra, the most famous NRDBMS

As its Web site says (http://cassandra.apache.org/) "the Apache Cassandra database is the right choice when you need scalability and high availability without compromising performance. Linear scalability and proven fault-tolerance on commodity hardware or cloud infrastructure make it the perfect platform for mission-critical data. Cassandra's support for replicating across multiple datacenters is best-in-class, providing lower latency for your users and the peace of mind of knowing that you can survive regional outages.

Cassandra's ColumnFamily data model offers the convenience of column indexes with the performance of log-structured updates, strong support for materialized views, and powerful built-in caching."

Basically, Cassandra is an open source distributed database management system, a NoSQL solution that was initially developed by Facebook. It is an Apache Software Foundation top-level project designed to handle very large amounts of data spread out across many commodity servers while providing a highly available service with no single point of failure. Jeff Hammerbacher, who led the Facebook Data team at the time, has described Cassandra as a BigTable data model running on an Amazon Dynamo-like infrastructure.

Cassandra provides a structured key-value store with tuneable consistency. Keys map to multiple values, which are grouped into column families. The column families are fixed when a Cassandra database is created, but columns can be added to a family at any time. Furthermore, columns are added only to specified keys, so different keys can have different numbers of columns in any given family.

The values from a column family for each key are stored together. This makes Cassandra a hybrid data management system between a column-oriented DBMS and a row-oriented store. Additional features include:

using the BigTable way of modelling, eventual consistency, and the Gossip protocol, a master-master way of serving read and write requests inspired by Amazon's Dynamo.

Conclusion

Non-relational database management model seems to be definitely the way ahead. It is brilliantly showing more flexibility and more general capabilities than the traditional model in terms of easy, rapid and rational management of impressive amount of data, without too many limitations and implications. Big companies that switched their database management to NRDBMS, moreover, demonstrated that from the strategic advantages point of view, non-relational databases exploit corporate digital assets in a very solid and performing way, especially when particular attention is paid to some consistency light problems that still are present in this new system, but that will disappear in the next future due to the better research performances incoming in this field.

I am still working on this subject, I would suggest you then to visit my Web sites to keep yourself updated about any news about my works:

- www.facebook.com/nicola.amato.scrittore
- nicola-amato.blogspot.it
- www.amazon.it/Nicola-Amato/e/B0058FNDFQ/

Thanks for your interest in this matter.

Bibliography

- Amazon, (2011). *Amazon SimpleDB Overview*. [Online]. Available at: http://aws.amazon.com/simpledb [Accessed 6 July 2011].

- Cassandra, (2009). *Apache Cassandra Project*. [Online]. Available at: http://cassandra.apache.org [Accessed 6 July 2011].

- Creswell, J.W., (2002). Research Design: Qualitative, Quantitative, and Mixed Methods Approaches. Middlesborough: Sage.

- Gajda, K.L., Hess, B.A., Kemp, J.A.H., Lewis, J.J., Thorpe, R.T. (2002).

Method and system for improved access to non-relational databases. U.S. Pat. 6502088. Available at:

http://www.patentgenius.com/patent/6502088.html
[Accessed 4 July 2011].

- Google, (2011). *Google App Engine Developer's Guide.*. [Online]. Available at:
  http://code.google.com/appengine/docs
  [Accessed 6 July 2011].

- Habeeb, M., (2010). A Developer's Guide to Amazon SimpleDB. Boston: Addison-Wesley Professional.

- Hewitt, E., (2010). Cassandra: The Definitive Guide.
  Sebastopol, CA: O'reilly Media Inc.

- Leavitt, N., (2010). Will NoSQL Databases Live Up to Their Promise?

Computer journal 43 (2), pp.12-14. Available through:

IEEE Xplore digital library [Accessed 4 July 2011].

- Oates, B., (2006). Researching Information Systems and

  Computing. Middlesborough: Sage.

- Rasmus, D.W., (2008). Building Strategic Advantage

  Through IT. Redmond, WA: Microsoft Corporation.

- Reese, G., (2009). Cloud Application Architectures:
  Building Applications and Infrastructure in the
  Cloud. Sebastopol, CA: O'reilly Media Inc.

- Roebuck, K., (2011). Storing and managing big data -

  NoSQL, Hadoop and more: High-impact Strategies -
  What You Need to Know: Definitions, Adoptions,
  Impact, Benefits, Maturity, Vendors. Sidney:
  Emereo Pty Limited.

- Sanderson, D., (2009). Programming Google App Engine:
  Build and Run Scalable Web Apps on Google's Infrastructure. Sebastopol, CA: O'reilly Media Inc.

- Stonebraker, M., (2010). SQL databases v. NoSQL databases. *Magazine Communications of the ACM* 53 (4), pp.10-11. Available through: ACM digital library
  [Accessed 4 July 2011].

- Taniar, D., Rusu, L.I., (2009). Strategic Advancements in Utilizing Data Mining and Warehousing Technologies: New Concepts and Developments. Hershey, Pennsylvania: Information Science Publishing.

- Tiwari, S., (2011). Professional NoSQL. London: Wrox Press.

- Vicknair, C., Macias, M., Zhao, Z., Nan, X., Chen, Y. Wilkins, D. (2010). A Comparison of a graph database and a relational database: a data provenance perspective. In: University of Mississippi, *48th Annual Southeast Regional Conference.* Oxford, MS, USA 15-17 April 2010. New York: ACM. Available through: ACM digital library [Accessed 4 July 2011].

About the author

Nicola Amato is an audio-visual and multimedia communication technologist, IT and ICT expert. He has been a university professor of "Elusive techniques of communication and hidden writings" in the university Insubria of Varese (Italy), and currently is lecturer of "Database design for Information Management" at University of Alberta (Canada).